Total MindBody Training

A Guide to

Peak Athletic Performance

D1545384

Total MindBody Training

A Guide to
Peak Athletic Performance

by
Jacob H. Jordan, M.D.

TP   Turtle Press   Hartford

TOTAL MINDBODY TRAINING

Photographs courtesy of Jacob H. Jordan, M.D.
Cover Design by Pamela Beebe

To contact the author or to order additional copies of this book:

Turtle Press
401 Silas Deane Hwy
P.O. Box 290206
Wethersfield CT 06129-0206

Library of Congress Card Catalog Number 94-46304

ISBN   1-880336-06-5

First Edition

Library of Congress Cataloguing in Publication Data

Jordan, Jacob H. 1958 -
      Total mindbody training : a guide to peak athletic
      performance / by Jacob H. Jordan. - - 1st ed.
            p.   cm.
      Includes index.
      ISBN 1-880336-06-5
      1. Martial arts - - Psychological aspects. 2. Physical
    education and training. 3. Mind and body. I. Title.
      II. Title: Total mind-body training.
      GV1102.7.P75J67   1995
         796.8 - - dc20   94-46304

Contents

Introduction

This book is for martial artists and athletes who are dedicated to the continual improvement of their chosen art. *Mind-Body Training* draws the athlete to this task by providing a step by step training system designed from a goal directed, Western mind-set rather than from the Eastern philosophies traditionally inherent in martial arts practice.

The past two decades have yielded significant advances in peak performance athletic training methods. While these methods originated in the Eastern block Olympic training camps, the technologies have now spread to most major Western sports. Despite the effectiveness of these tactics, rarely are they applied to martial arts practice. I believe that these new technologies have failed to make inroads into the training halls because Eastern training methods and philosophy are so deeply ingrained in martial arts practice. Some instructors would consider it heresy to diverge from the traditional training ways. In an attempt to preserve tradition, the Eastern teachings have become roadblocks to newly evolving training strategies. While the classic Zen and Taoist teachings have great merit, many Western athletes find Eastern philosophy hard to understand and difficult to effectively apply to their training. The problem is rooted in the differences between Eastern and Western thought.

No one familiar with Eastern cultures would argue that there are vast differences between Eastern and Western thought. Western logic is based on linear, cognitive reasoning while Eastern thought tends to be more intuitive. For the practitioner trained in Western reasoning to fully comprehend many of the Eastern concepts requires a leap from the Western intellect. Unfortunately, most athletes fall short in this attempt and revert back to familiar, cognitive based training methods. Applied Eastern philosophy remains ambiguous and hard to grasp for most Westerners.

Most top Western athletes know nothing of Zen concepts. Even so, upon questioning, many describe having experienced states similar to the "No Mind" and "Selfless" states sought by the Eastern disciplines. These athletes achieved the Eastern performance goals more by accident than by purposeful strategy. The mind-body training techniques in this book comprise a step by step approach toward these same goals by a path congruent with the Western mind-set.

This is not a martial arts instruction manual—no sparring techniques or katas are presented. I leave those teachings to your instructor. In the following pages you will find no Zen koans (riddles) to ponder and point the way. You will not be told how to flow with the life force or divide your being into two separate selves as is common in today's popular sports psychology. Mind-body training does not aspire to the lofty goal of spiritual enlightenment. The purpose of this book is to lift the veil of mysticism and ambiguity surrounding the mental aspects of martial arts training by providing you with easy, applicable techniques to realize your potential.

Goals and Motivational Force

the foundation

The attrition rate for martial arts students is extremely high. Depending on the school, an average of less than one in two hundred beginning students reach the level of black belt. I have witnessed many students with exceptional abilities fail to approach their potential because they omitted the first and most important step of achievement - goal setting.

Before any athletic training regimen can be successfully instituted, goals and motivational force must be established. Problems arise in this area because of frequent misinterpretations of Zen and Taoist teaching as applied to athletic training regimens. The teachings of the Eastern disciplines commonly put forth in

Western programs rarely express goal directed training. In one martial arts school, I was informed that ambition and the process of *trying* to achieve goals enhance the ego, thus creating the antithesis of the selfless state desired in Zen training. This is an unfortunate misconception and yet another example of the misunderstanding of Eastern concepts by the Western intellect.

All successful people in any endeavor are goal directed. Goals establish the blueprint to keep you on course throughout your training. Goals provide a clear measure of progress. Unfortunately, few martial arts students heed this important lesson. Whenever I expound upon the importance of goal setting and motivation, at least one half of the students in the class immediately lose interest and get a defocused, glazed look in their eyes. Invariably most fail to recognize that all the conditioning and training tools known are of no use without clear goals which direct and motivate the practitioner.

Perform each technique with a clear goal in mind.

The Training Journal

For any serious goal directed training program, a training journal is essential. The journal will help keep you on course toward your chosen goals. In it you will record your goals, your motivation, your training plans, your successes and your setbacks. It will be the record of your progress. This journal will be a valuable training companion. I suggest that your journal be bound since loose pages are easily misplaced. I have found that a nine and one half by six inch spiral notebook works well for this purpose. Obtain a suitable journal prior to proceeding with the goal setting exercises in the following section.

Establish the Target

Everyone has held ambitions that were never realized. I frequently witness talented martial artists reach a plateau in their abilities, soon to become bored and move on to another sport. The most common initial difficulty practitioners face stems from the absence of a well-defined set of goals that inspire. As the saying goes "you can't hit a target unless you have one." The average practitioner wastes valuable training time in workouts without focus. They come to the training hall, socialize, execute a set pattern of basic techniques, engage in a few minutes of sparring and socialize again before leaving. In this fashion of training, improvement is haphazard at best. Clear, precise goals direct the mind which in turn directs the body to tap more potential and use physical resources more fully. Goals define your path of action.

In the early stages of martial arts training, setting goals is usually straight forward, based on the practice guidelines set forth by the belt rank system. Each martial arts style has certain techniques that must be mastered to qualify for the next rank. As you advance to higher levels of training, your goals may ascend beyond style requirements and become increasingly more self directed.

Regardless of your level of proficiency, every training session should have a precise goal whether it is to perfect a kata or to improve the speed of your roundhouse kick. Always be specific when stating your goals. The more clearly you define your goals, the more power they give you. When stating your goals, stay away from relative terms such as "being the best" or "improving." These statements are ambiguous and will fail to adequately direct your training. Clarity provides the focus that keeps you on the straight and narrow towards achievement.

Exercise 1A
Establishing Goals

The first step in your training program is to list your desired goals in your training journal. Be as clear and precise as possible. For example, do not simply list "high kicks" as a goal. Instead, be descriptive using language that is motivating to you personally. You may choose "roundhouse kick with perfect form, lightning fast at head level." Be specific!

After listing the desired goals in your journal, examine each goal closely. Seeing the goal in print often assists you in making certain distinctions. Is this a reasonable goal? While it is good to have goals that challenge you, be realistic about your abilities. If you are seventy years of age, winning the nationals may not be a wise goal to pursue. On the deepest level, you must *know* that you can accomplish the goal. Strong belief plays a major role in the accomplishment of any endeavor.

Setting Goals Effectively

1. Be specific and clear when choosing your goals

2. Choose personally motivating words and phrases

3. Write goals down in your training journal

4. Be challenging but realistic

5. Know that you can achieve each goal

The Power of Belief

The human body is a remarkable instrument that responds to belief. More often than not, the body will adapt over time to the expectations of its owner. In medicine there is a well studied phenomenon that demonstrates the power of belief systems. It is known as the placebo effect. This concept has been proven repeatedly and is the standard for evaluating the efficacy of new drugs. To illustrate this phenomenon, a patient in pain is given a sugar pill but told that the pill contains a powerful narcotic that will alleviate his discomfort. Over one third of the patients will experience as much pain relief as if the actual narcotic had been given. If you administer a stimulant but tell the patient it is a powerful sedative, many people respond by becoming drowsy. The patient's physiology will conform to the belief system supplied by the physician.

The same type of phenomenon is seen routinely in athletic endeavors. Several world records fall every year, more because of changing beliefs about what is humanly possible than through improved training strategy. Give your body a reasonable expectation backed by complete faith in your ability and your body will respond. You must believe with all your heart that you can achieve your chosen goal and expect its attainment!

After your target has been identified, the next step is to charge your goal with the motivational energy needed to bring it to reality.

Motivating Force

Nothing sabotages potential champions more often than a lack of motivational fuel at a critical point in training. Motivation is not found and it is not a genetically bestowed gift - it must be actively created. The first step to create lasting motivation is to take a close look at the goals you have established and get a clear understanding of the driving force behind your choice of these goals. You must have a strong *why* and *what* behind the desire to achieve your goals. In other words, *why* is this goal important to you and *what* will be the benefit if it is attained. The importance of the answers to these questions cannot be overemphasized as your reasons will probably determine if you succeed.

I always ask my students what prompted them to take up the martial arts. I usually get stock answers such as "to defend myself," "to lose weight," "to tone muscles," "to impress my friends" and "to increase endurance". Occasionally I get a spiritual seeker who answers "to find myself," or some other new age slogan. These answers all lack the essential element needed to create exceptional motivation. They lack the specificity and emotional depth needed to individualize the goal and to ignite the drive for personal development.

Goals are all about self-image. Strong motivation that will not fail in times of fatigue and boredom usually originates from self directed or inward goals. This is to say that the grounds that shape the basis of your motivation are founded on how your goals benefit your personal development rather than being dependent on some external factor. For example, if you are learning martial art skills simply to be able to defeat a particular person, you will find this to be a hollow reason when the training gets tough. If that person moves away or is no longer in the picture, your motivation essentially goes with him. The same thing holds true if you are trying to impress your friends or make your parents proud. On the other hand, if you are learning the art to become a more confident, secure individual, your enthusiasm is much more likely to hang with you through the tough times. The highest successes are achieved by those who utilize goals to assist them to evolve towards the type of person they wish to be.

The second step to creating motivation is to personalize your goal. This is accomplished by expanding your self-image to include the desired goal. You must view yourself as a person that has accomplished your chosen challenge. If you wholeheartedly identify with your current belt rank, attaining the next level rank will be difficult. Unless you first incorporate your goal into your self image, you become stuck in your current belief system.

In your mind's eye, see yourself bringing your goal to fruition. How would you feel about yourself if this was achieved? How would your muscles feel performing the desired goal? What would you know that you may not know now? How would others respond to you? What attributes does this goal give you? Take a moment to sense how this feels. Does the feeling excite you? Is this the direction that you wish your life to take? Concentrate on what intrigues you or what you love most about your chosen goal. Does it motivate you to train? If so, you are on your way.

The third step in creating motivation is to always be appreciative of what you have accomplished and the potential you possess.   In my practice as a physician, I regularly encounter people whose physical disabilities create enormous obstacles to proficiency in any sport. When I see this, I realize that my practice of karate is a privilege to be cherished. I have an opportunity to practice skills that can enhance me personally - an opportunity that many people do not have. Recognizing this fact never fails to inspire me to continue working towards my ideal. It is this process of self-improvement and progress, rather than the actual goal, that bestows satisfaction and motivation.

Steps to Creating Motivation

1. Assign a "Why" (importance) and "What" (benefit) to each goal.

2. Personalize your goal with images & emotion.

3. Appreciate your accomplishments and cherish your potential.

Exercise 1B
Creating Motivation

In your training journal, next to each goal, write the *Why* and *What* sustaining your goal. *Why* is this goal important and *What* will its achievement do for you. This may take paragraphs or may be summed up in a few meaningful words. What attributes will the goal provide you? How would you feel about yourself if the goal was realized? Use language that is personally inspiring, remembering that motivation flows from feelings, not analysis.

The Time Factor

After your goals and motivational force have been established, the next step is to plan your successes. Each goal should be broken down into increments that have a high probability of attainment within a relatively short span of time. It is important to stay realistic in your time estimate. If you are a beginner, do not expect to earn your black belt in four months. Beginners, in their enthusiasm, tend to be overly optimistic and underestimate the time required to reach certain levels of proficiency. This only leads to frustration when they fall behind schedule. On the other hand, experienced martial artists characteristically overestimate time requirements and in doing so, often undershoot their potential.

I recommend shooting for short term goals that can be reasonably achieved within three to eight weeks with conscientious training. In this stepwise fashion, achieving your ultimate goal is the culmination of multiple smaller successes. Dividing the objective into a series of successes keeps the practitioner oriented to the *process* of achievement. Your final goal is not merely a promised reward in a far off future, it is actively being created at this moment. By being process oriented, your attention focuses on the current action which in turn enhances your performance and accelerates progress towards your objective. There is nothing like the feelings of achievement to fuel your motivation and desire for the further advancement of your skills.

Always remain flexible when making goals. Goal setting is an evolving process. As one goal is achieved, it will often crystallize your next step for you. You may find that your original long-term goals change many times throughout the course of training, as more insight is developed. Try to judge whether the effort and time necessary to reach the chosen goal will justify its usefulness and satisfaction. By frequently evaluating your goals in this manner you can avoid wasting valuable time and feelings of burnout.

Exercise 1C
Setting the Time Table

In your training journal, divide each goal into attainable, incremental steps. Each mini-goal should take at least three weeks but no more than six to eight weeks to achieve.

Plan to Action

The final phase in the preparation for training is to determine the steps required to achieve your goal in the desired time frame.   In this section, you will list the physical abilities and skills required to accomplish your goal such as stretching, diet, endurance training, etc. The skills are then placed in the time frame allotted for completion. To illustrate, your training journal may look something like this:

Training Plan:

Goals Roundhouse Kick, head level, lightning fast

Motivation Increased flexibility. Formidable sparring opponent. Feelings of empowerment. Gratifying accomplishment. Powerful, respected martial artist.

Time frame to completion 4 weeks

Week One: Daily stretching Hip twists X 20. Visualization X 10 minutes. Roundhouse kick solar plexus level X 20 each leg.

Week Two: Daily stretching. Hip twists X 20 Visualization X 10 minutes. Bagwork: Roundhouse Kick X 20 versus heavy bag, both legs. Roundhouse Kick chest level X 20 each leg.

Week Three: Daily stretching. Daily visualization. Bagwork: Roundhouse Kick vs. heavy bag X 20 both legs. Speedwork: Roundhouse Kick, neck level, X 5 in air without letting foot touch floor. Repeat X 10 each leg.

Week Four: Daily stretch. Daily visualization. Bagwork: Roundhouse Kick vs. heavy bag, head level, X 20 each leg. Speedwork: Roundhouse Kick, head level, X 5 without letting foot touch floor. Repeat X 10 each leg.

This is only an example. It is not important how you organize your training journal as long as it makes sense to you.

Pitfalls

For years I have heard martial artists boast objectives such as "someday I will be able to perform a full split." Needless to say, someday never arrives for most of these individuals. Procrastination arises from failing to focus on your goals and ignoring your time frame. It is a deadly stumbling block for all achievers.

Even the most devoted of martial artists have encountered problems with procrastination at some time during training. We have all experienced times when the easy chair seems to have a much stronger gravitational pull than the training hall. At times we have all avoided techniques that are particularly taxing for us. Once inertia sets in, it often requires momentous effort to get back on the path of conscientious training.

The majority of instructors and coaches I have encountered view this problem as a character flaw of the practitioner. Procrastination is frowned upon as lack of dedication, absence of discipline and failure of will. No one would argue that discipline is required in martial arts practice or that the most successful are usually the most disciplined. Unfortunately, the view of procrastination as merely a weakness considers the problem from an angle which offers no solution. Lack of motivation occurs when a goal no longer holds immediate importance. What is missing at that moment is not discipline, but enthusiasm and desire.

In such an instance, a training journal can be quite helpful. When your motivation is waning, review the basis of your motives written in exercise 1B. How would you feel if the goal was accomplished? Does the goal still excite you? Perhaps another path to the same goal would be more motivating.

If you continue to find yourself drifting and your motivation declining, its time to reevaluate your priorities. Possibly the goal is no longer worth the effort of its achievement. For example, many older martial artists have difficulty executing high kicks. Frequently one half of the workout is spent performing stretching exercises to allow head level kicks. One must ask if this is a proper goal and the most efficient use of workout time. A more appropriate goal may be to perfect waist high kicks with follow-up hand techniques to the head and neck. You must always remain flexible while developing your goals and training regimens. If physical limitations imposed by age or injury prohibit certain techniques, you may consider changing to a martial arts style that stresses your strengths. Remember that successful people always look for what works *for them.*

Overtraining

Occasionally, expecting too much of yourself in a short span of time can lead to overtraining. Overtraining results in sore muscles, fatigue and lack of motivation. The physical manifestations of overtraining lead to diminished performance. This can be frustrating for athletes who often respond by redoubling their efforts and driving themselves harder, resulting in further loss in performance. In this instance, you need to break the training cycle and relax. Sometimes a few days off are all that is required to restore the drive to continue. Don't take the do or die approach! If you are a little late on your time schedule, it is not the end of the world. Remember to be flexible and enjoy the process of goal achievement.

Motivational assistance can also be obtained from other people. My first instructor was a dynamic individual. He never failed to inspire and drive me to give my best effort. The value of such a coach or training partner cannot be overestimated. It is easy for the dedicated athlete to get caught in the middle of an ambitious training program and lose the overall perspective. An experienced coach can act as an impartial observer to point out training problems and keep you on the path of healthful training. If you find yourself lagging behind your schedule and not performing up to your expectations, a strong, enthusiastic coach or training partner may be just the spark you need to rekindle your training drive.

Performance

through physiology

I always benefit from attending competitive athletic events. Competitive tournaments provide a wide variety of lessons for the spectator with a keen eye for detailed observation. While watching the participants, one can identify and study all of the physical manifestations of the peak performance state as well as its antithesis. Some competitors appear nervous or fearful, while others walk with a relaxed air of confidence.

After attending several martial arts tournaments, you can readily identify the top competitors simply by their demeanor. These individuals exude a calm confidence. Their movements appear fluid and effortless. These physical qualities radiate that they are winners. Whether fearful, nervous or confident, competitors actively create their appearance as well as their performance. Their internal representations of themselves in relation to the event are apparent in their physiology.

I can still vividly recall the first time I was called upon to spar another student in front of the entire karate class. It was over twenty five years ago but the event is indelibly etched in my mind. I was tense and tremulous, fearing that I would be kicked and punched into submission or worse, look foolish. My opponent took one look at this hunched over, stiff yellow belt and recognized an easy victim. I had lost the match before it had started.

Contrast this physical message with that of the top tournament competitors described previously. Their physical poise expresses self-assurance and proficiency. The confidence and power demonstrated by their demeanor actually takes something away from their opponents before any physical competition begins.

The poise and winning attitude demonstrated by top competitors is most often the product of confidence gained from years of training and accomplishment. Of course not everyone has such experiences from which to draw. Well before he became a household name, Mohammed Ali was known for his confident nature and *cocky* attitude. He knew that he was the best and would tell anyone who would listen. Later in his career he spoke to this point. To paraphrase, Ali said "in order to become a champion, you must first look and act like a champion." The fastest path to this goal is to train your physiology to take on the traits of a winner.

Unshakable confidence characterized by fluid movements and calmness is the most powerful tool in sports psychology. If your opponent believes you to be superior, your chances of winning increase proportionately. Physical appearance and the image you project are powerful tools. However, your physical state is much more than simply a tool for *appearing* proficient. A proper physical state is the cornerstone to optimal mental, emotional and physical performance.

Mind, Physiology and Emotion

Everyone would agree that the mind directs the body. What most people fail to realize is that mind-body interaction is a two way street. Are you skeptical? Remember a time when you were dead tired and forced yourself to go to the training hall. The first few warm-up exercises were tortuous, however, after a few minutes your state began to change. A new surge of energy appeared and techniques began to flow more effortlessly. You became more focused, your spirits improved, and the workout became enjoyable. What transpired was that your physical movements instructed your mind to be alert and tap more energy reserves. Your mental state was changed by your physical actions.

Changing your physiology can also inhibit unresourceful emotions such as fear and anxiety. I began studying karate at the age of nine in a very traditional shorin-ryu school. Sparring was rigorous and often the blows had little control. When struck hard and soundly defeated by my adult peers as a young practitioner, I often experienced an overwhelming sense of frustration and discouragement. Fortunately my instructor was well aware of the power of proper physical state. Whenever children in the class became frustrated or dejected, my instructor would immediately force a change in physiology. He would make us stand up and stretch, hold our shoulders back and chin up while taking deep, diaphragmatic breaths. Occasionally he would shake us heartily and laugh as to say "don't be so serious!" Rarely did these measures fail to quickly reverse the negative emotions and restore the young student's sense of self-control. A positive emotional state was elicited by adopting a confident physiology.

The benefits of proper body mechanics cannot be overemphasized. When fatigued or anxious, most practitioners attempt to psyche themselves up strictly through mental commands. To try to change your outlook or muster energy through sheer will alone is extremely difficult and rarely successful. The mind seems to have an agenda of its own. When an individual is fearful or anxious, even constant, positive affirmations have little effect. Unless these commands translate into a change in physiology there will be no significant change in performance.

Mind, physiology and emotion are inextricably connected. Altering one will immediately produce a complementary change in the other two. Among mind, physiology and emotion, physiology is by far the most responsive to willful commands. By learning to control physiology through appropriate, positive physical actions, you can then direct mind and emotion to more resourceful states.

Exercise 2A
Peak Physiology

Now is the time to experiment with your physiology. Right now, stand up and stretch. Stand as tall as you can, hold your shoulders back, your chin up, and take three deep, cleansing breaths. Do you feel more energetic? More alert? More confident? Note the change in state that can be attained by merely changing your physical actions and posture.

Modeling

I once heard a story about an actor who appeared unexpectedly at a large martial arts school claiming to be a high ranking black belt from another city. He was so convincing that he was allowed to review the class and even give pointers to first and second degree black belts. He had only six months of martial arts training! By modeling the traits of a proficient karateka so well, he even fooled the head instructor of the school. Despite his fraudulent presentation, this is an excellent example of what a skillful modeler can accomplish.

Whether learning how to take our first steps as an infant or receiving instruction in the martial arts, we all learn by the same method, that of modeling. We watch our instructors and attempt to emulate their movements, while, in the process, expanding our own abilities.

The first step down the path of peak physiology involves modeling but in a more comprehensive sense than usually practiced. Instead of merely imitating movements, one must adopt the model's entire physiology. Act as if you are actually the person being modeled. Assume the instructor's posture, rhythm of movement, even their breathing pattern and facial expressions. In essence, use your entire physiology for performing even the most basic of techniques. By integrating your physiology into each technique, the correct neuromuscular connections required to perform the technique imprint more quickly. When you imitate all of the instructor's physical characteristics, you get an idea of what they sense when performing the action. You receive the same physiologic message the instructor creates. In this way you experience *how it feels* to perform the technique well from a whole body perspective rather than only going through the motions. This *quality of sensation* is what you draw upon to reproduce the same result in the future.

While modeling is a natural way to learn, in my opinion, it should only be used in the initial learning process. I have never seen a person reach their full potential solely through modeling. During the early 1970's, martial arts tournaments were full of young Bruce Lee imitators. There were always several at any large tournament who could emulate his posture, facial expressions, basic movement and even his distinctive vocalizations. It was comical to watch all of the "Bruce Lees" prancing around putting on quite a show. I soon realized that none of these imitators ever made it to the finals. Perhaps Bruce Lee's formula for peak physiology was not the key to their own. As your skill increases and your techniques evolve, you must make the transition from modeling to the development of your own style and physiology for peak performance. The remainder of this book is dedicated to this process.

Whole body modeling ingrains correct technique.

Exercise 2B
Sensing the Body

Choose a physical activity that you feel confident performing. For a martial artist, this may be a reverse punch, a backfist strike, or a side kick. Perform the action not only concentrating on the primary movement, but paying attention to *how your body feels* during the action. For example, if you chose a backfist strike as the action, concentrate not only on the motion of the arm and the shoulder but sense your facial expression, which muscles are tense and which are relaxed, how your hips twist and the position of your feet. Pay attention to all aspects of your physiology as you feel the technique performed. In this way you integrate *the sensation* of performing well into your entire physiology. Once grasped, this sensation can then be carried over and applied to other actions. Practice this exercise to become acclimated to performing all techniques from a whole body perspective.

The Flow State

Most martial artists have experienced moments when they sensed that they were performing optimally. It may have lasted only a few moments or several hours. Take a minute and recall a time when the workout was flowing and techniques seemed effortless. This does not have to relate directly to martial arts but could be any physical activity. You were calm yet alert, feeling totally in synch with your body movements and surroundings. This experience is what sports analysts describe as the "flow state."

Top athletes in every sport recognize the flow state although the label has changed through the years. Being *hot*, *in the groove*, *in the cocoon*, *being on* and *in the zone* all describe the same state of optimal performance. In the flow state the athlete is comfortable and relaxed even while executing physically rigorous techniques. There is a notable absence of any anxiety, tension, worry, or distraction. The practitioner perceives a sense of control and a distinct inner knowing that everything is as it should be regardless of what is taking place around him. Once experienced fully, the sensation is never forgotten. The flow state characterizes the epitome of a rewarding athletic experience.

When experiencing the flow state, the athlete has the impression of performing at the peak of his abilities and occasionally, even beyond present abilities. It is sometimes described as though an almost magical force originating outside one's self has been temporarily harnessed. I believe this sensation of peak performance to be the foundation for the concept of

Ki (chi) or life force energy. This concept has always been recognized in Zen training as well as other Eastern disciplines, however it has always been portrayed as having somewhat mystical qualities.

Top athletes often have the ability to access this peak performance state at key moments during competition. These are the "clutch" players that always come through when the pressure is on. By studying these athletes, sports psychologists have identified physiologic cues distinct to each individual athlete that appear to induce the flow state. While every individual has their own physiologic triggers for attaining the flow state, the ingredients are always the same. By knowing the factors involved, anyone can formulate their own peak performance physiology by adjusting the quality and the combinations of the various physical factors. Fortunately, the factors number only three: breath, rhythm, and quality of movement.

Diaphragmatic Breathing

We have seen that mind and body are intertwined. Just as the mind moves the body, the body can move the mind. The key aspect of physiologic control of the mind is breath control. Respiration is truly the mirror of the psycho-physiologic state. While many people have developed a proverbial "poker face" with little clues to their emotions portrayed as facial expressions, their true mental state is always reflected in their breathing pattern. Anger is characterized by rapid breaths with forced exhalations. Anxiety is demonstrated by an erratic, fitful breathing pattern with breaths taken from high in the chest. While respiration reflects your emotional and physiologic state, it can also be utilized to change the state within seconds.

In the Western world we have been taught to breathe from high in the chest. This stems from the Western ideal of proper posture characterized by a puffed out chest with the stomach sucked in. Take a moment and assume this position. Notice how much energy is expended maintaining this posture. Hold this position for any length of time and soon you will notice how much tension is present. Maintain this position for fifteen to twenty minutes and fatigue will soon follow. While the martial arts teaches us to breathe from the abdomen, with states of tension, fear and anxiety, most students soon revert back to the shallow thoracic (chest) breaths which serve only to perpetuate sub-optimal states. In order to fully comprehend proper breath control, the mechanics of respiration must be understood.

The diaphragm is the primary muscle of respiration. This is the large, flat muscle separating the abdominal from the chest cavities. The diaphragm contracts thus lengthening the chest cavity creating a vacuum which draws air into the lungs. The secondary or so called accessory muscles of respiration include the intercostal muscles (between the ribs), and to a lesser extent, the neck muscles. The accessory muscles function to increase the anterior-posterior diameter of the chest cavity as well as to lift and spread the rib cage. With good "Western" posture we use our accessory musculature to lift the chest. Using the accessory muscles without proper use of the diaphragm serves to keep air high in the chest and does not expand the lungs to their capacity. A normal thoracic breath draws only 500 to 700 cc of air in the average adult. This results in less efficient oxygen delivery to your circulatory system and subsequently less potential for physical action. On the other hand, a deep, abdominal breath typically draws 2500cc to 3000cc of air, expanding the entire lungs for optimal oxygen delivery.

With this background we can now approach the process of proper respiration. Normal, quiet respiration uses only the diaphragm. This is what is termed abdominal breathing. The chest is kept completely still and the accessory muscles are not utilized. This is the proper way to breathe. It is the way infants normally breathe before they become conditioned and are taught "proper posture." It is the way a cat or other predatory animal breathes when stealthily stalking game.

Breathing should be accomplished by allowing the abdomen to inflate like a balloon creating the sensation of air being pulled deep into the lower body. When you have reached a maximum comfortable breath, press the air even further down towards the pelvis by tensing the abdomen slightly. Expiration is then accomplished in a gradual, controlled manner. Keeping slight tension in the abdominal muscles, the air is slowly released. The accessory muscles should come into play only when winded, contracting only after a full diaphragmatic breath has been accomplished. The accessory muscles are then utilized to expand and lift the chest to more fully inflate the very top portions of the lungs.

All breathing should be done through the nose with the exception of when vocalizing as when a martial artist performs a kiai. Nose breathing is most efficient for oxygen delivery and preserves the moisture of the airways. This becomes extremely important when involved in lengthy, dehydrating workouts.

Proper respiration has four major benefits for the martial artist. First, through a neuro-physiologic feedback loop, it keeps the mind calm and "grounded." Just try to become extremely angry or hysterical while taking slow, deep, abdominal breaths. It simply cannot be done. In competitive or confrontational situations, some athletes become so anxious and hyperactive that they are bouncing off the walls. This is the sympathetic nervous system in action. An activated sympathetic nervous system releases a flood of adrenaline resulting in the "fight or flight" response. The adrenaline surge is taxing on both the body and the mind wasting enormous energy reserves. Deep, abdominal breathing with slight tension in the abdomen dampens the sympathetic response in favor of the parasympathetic nervous system. The parasympathetic nervous system fosters relaxation, lowering of the pulse, slowing of respiration and conservation of energy. You are then able to respond to a threat appropriately rather than reacting anxiously. The preservation of energy reserves with parasympathetic system dominance becomes very important in endurance activities.

Secondly, proper breathing allows superior oxygen exchange in the lungs resulting in improved muscle performance during activity requiring maximal effort. Third, keeping the breath low in the abdomen automatically keeps your center of gravity low for improved balance. The fourth and probably the most important quality of proper respiration is its ability to assist in keeping the mind focused on the present moment. This will be discussed in detail in Chapter Three.

Developing the habit of diaphragmatic breathing takes considerable practice. It has taken years to condition your breathing to your current pattern so don't expect miraculous changes overnight. It will take time to condition your body back to the normal respiration that it knew as an infant, but it will be well worth the effort.

Benefits of Proper Respiration

1. Calms the mind by calming the body

2. Allows superior oxygen exchange

3. Lowers the center of gravity for better balance

4. Enhances focus

Exercise 2C
Diaphragmatic Breathing

Step One: First we are going to experience chest breathing. Sit tall in your chair or stand while raising your shoulders and upper chest. Take a deep breath through your mouth, concentrating on expanding the chest as much as possible with your inhalation. Now expire and lower the chest. Notice how this feels.

Step Two: Now shift your attention to your lower abdomen. Take a deep breath through your nose allowing your abdomen to expand outward like a balloon while keeping your chest completely still. Let your shoulders hang and keep your neck totally relaxed. Just draw in enough air to comfortably expand the lungs. Try to press the air even further into the pelvis by tensing the abdomen slightly. Now slowly relax and release the air maintaining only slight tension in the abdominal muscles. Keep your chest still throughout the breath. Note how much less energy this requires than chest breathing. Continue your abdominal breaths for one to two minutes concentrating on nice, slow, deep inhalations. Note how calming and relaxing abdominal breathing is.

The Rhythm of Breath

While reading the previous paragraphs, hopefully you have taken the time to attempt several diaphragmatic breaths. While most people find this awkward at first, soon this type of respiration becomes quite relaxing and enjoyable. With practice it becomes natural to breathe in this manner while sitting or standing quietly. Most martial arts teach diaphragmatic breathing. Then why do most practitioners still maintain "chest" breathing? You will find it quite difficult to maintain deep, abdominal breaths when engaged in activities requiring maximum physical effort. Your breathing becomes erratic and will not hold its calming effect. What is missing and rarely taught in any school is the second part of proper breath control - rhythm.

When you watch any expert karateka performing kata or engaged in free sparring, their techniques seem to have a flowing rhythm. This is also seen in many other sports, however is most notable in long distance running, boxing, swimming and endurance activities. Most seasoned athletes have a familiar pattern of breathing developed over years of training. In many instances, the breathing pattern evolved without the athlete being consciously aware of it.

Your timing and rhythm of physical movement are intricately linked to your own natural body rhythms, that is your breathing and your heart beat. Most people immediately exclaim "but I don't even notice my heart beat!" While it is not usually in your conscious awareness, just ask anyone who has occasional skips in their heart rhythm if they are aware of their heart beat.

Nothing is noticed until the heart skips a beat and only then do they become acutely conscious of their heart rhythm. Your subconscious monitors these activities at all times below the level of your perceptions. Even at the subconscious level these physiologic patterns have a profound effect on your own timing and rhythm in physical activity.

Controlling your heartbeat is an ambitious task usually reserved for Indian yogis with years of meditation experience. The good news is you do not have run out and buy an Indian loincloth just yet. Keeping tension in the lower abdomen throughout the respiratory cycle stimulates the parasympathetic nervous system to keep the heart rate slow and regular. In addition, maintaining deep, abdominal breaths and a constant breathing rhythm supplies your heart with what it needs most, oxygen. Proper respiration stabilizes the heart rate and keeps the heart muscle functioning at peak capacity for any given situation.

So the next questions arises "how do I discover what my ideal breathing pattern is?" Actually this is a case where your breathing pattern has to find you. I would start with the basic breathing pattern of the boxer which is two short inhalations followed by one exhalation. Remember not to lose the abdominal breathing techniques that were learned in the previous section! Experiment with this pattern while performing techniques or a kata. With time your pattern will settle on its own to some variation of the original pattern. My own pattern is two short inhalations followed by two short exhalations. I find that my techniques have a more natural, flowing rhythm with this pattern of breathing. Remember to keep slight tension in the abdominal muscles at all times throughout the respiration cycle. With time and practice you will see remarkable improvements in your rhythm and your timing through the techniques of proper breathing. You will also find that your endurance improves significantly for you now breathe in a manner that allows more efficient oxygen delivery.

Breathing rhythm is best developed during simple exercises such as brisk walking.

Exercise 2D
Your Breathing Pattern

Try performing a familiar physical activity using the techniques of abdominal breathing with your chosen breathing pattern. You may perform a kata or choose something less complex such as jumping jacks or jogging. I usually suggest something simple such as brisk walking which everyone can do without training. During the activity, concentrate only on your abdominal breaths and your breathing pattern remembering to breathe through your nose. Try to maintain the breathing pattern throughout the activity and sense how your movements begin to become rhythmically timed to your respiration. For example, with brisk walking you may apply the basic breathing pattern in the following manner; two short inhalations with two steps (one with each inhalation) followed by one step with one short, forceful exhalation. Experiment with different respiratory patterns and choose the one that feels most naturally in synch with the rhythm of your movements.

There will be situations when you are forced to stray from your breathing pattern. Practicing the rhythm conscientiously until it becomes natural will ensure that the pattern returns automatically without requiring your attention.

Quality of Movement

The third factor entering into the physiologic equation of peak performance is the quality of your movements. Muscle movement and coordination are incredibly complex processes bringing into play numerous neuro-physiologic components. To simplify this complex interaction, we will deal with one primary factor of movement, muscle tension.

In my early training in martial arts, my instructor would lead the class through drills in which the object was to perform all of the techniques while keeping as relaxed as possible. If we tensed at any time, my instructor would tap us firmly or squeeze our muscles saying "loose, like a rag doll." As a young karateka I thought these exercises were of questionable benefit and actually somewhat humorous. I appreciated the worth of these sessions after watching videos of a young Mohammed Ali in one of his early boxing matches. Here was a fighter who had mastered the art of relaxation in action. Many times he would let his arms dangle just like the proverbial rag doll only to throw a devastating punch with lightening speed. "Float like a butterfly and sting like a bee" was an apt description of this man's ability to relax during a fight.

If there is one attribute that all so called natural athletes have in common, it is their apparent ability to look relaxed while performing difficult movements. Fluid movements appear effortless and graceful. Regardless of the style, a martial artist who has mastered fluid movement is awe inspiring to watch. What keeps the average athlete from achieving this is muscle tension.

Muscle Tension

Muscle tension is the enemy of all fluid movement and true power. Most people are amazed at how much tension is normally carried in their bodies once they become aware of it. Stress is stored in the form of tension in the neck, back, chest and facial muscles causing rigidity and lack of all suppleness. This continuous tension is a considerable drain on the athlete, wasting enormous amounts of physical and mental energy.

The musculoskeletal system of human limbs consists of opposing muscles surrounding joints. For example, the biceps and the triceps muscles oppose each other in the arm as the quadriceps and hamstring muscles oppose each other in the leg. If both sets of opposing muscles in a limb are contracting because of chronic tension, movements are erratic, slow and lack power. You are literally working against yourself. Therefore the key to true power and speed is the relaxation of muscles not actively involved in the execution of the technique.

When involved in physical activity, all muscles not in use should be totally relaxed. This is not as easy as it sounds. To relax in the midst of a vigorous sparring session seems like suicide. However, relaxation improves your response time considerably, sometimes even doubling the speed of a technique. Since power is directly related to speed, your power also increases significantly.

Opposing muscle tension acts as a brake, slowing the technique execution and stealing power. Even the subtlest degree of muscle tension in an antagonistic (opposing) muscle can have adverse effects on timing and movements requiring fine coordination. Releasing this tension also conserves energy which can now be utilized constructively for training endeavors.

Proper breathing and relaxation allow movements to flow naturally.

Muscle Relaxation

The first step to proper relaxation is simply noting how much tension you normally carry in your body. Consider your facial muscles. Right at this moment, make a conscious attempt to relax all of your facial muscles. Make your face totally soft and relaxed just letting the skin hang on the facial bones. Relax your jaw letting it rest comfortably. See how much tension was present just in the process of reading this book? The facial muscles carry significant tension any time there is emotion. Many people find that by totally relaxing their facial muscles and taking a few deep diaphragmatic breaths, the rest of the body settles and relaxes.

Take a moment now to concentrate on your neck, shoulders, and back muscles. Because of chronic stress and maintenance of proper "Western" posture with shoulders back and chest held high, considerable tension is carried in these muscles. The first goal to proper relaxation is to break this cycle of chronic, long-standing tension. Concentrate first on tensing your neck muscles and shoulders hard to get a sense of what tight contraction feels like. Also contract your trapezius muscles by forcefully shrugging your shoulders. Tense these areas hard and hold for five seconds, then relax. Just let these muscles go limp and concentrate on these areas becoming totally flaccid like jello. See how good it feels to relax? Perform this exercise of tensing and relaxing for all the muscles in the body including the hands, arms, chest, back, stomach, pelvis buttocks, and legs. Remain relaxed for at least thirty seconds, breathing slowly with deep, abdominal breaths.

After this is accomplished, perform a few techniques concentrating on keeping these areas relaxed during execution. Most people notice significant improvements in technique fluidity after the areas of chronic tension have been removed.

Always remember to keep slight tension in your lower abdominal muscles. Keeping these muscles slightly tensed will always keep you centered on your breathing for proper abdominal breaths and proper rhythm. Proper breathing in turn enhances the overall relaxation of the other muscles. You use your abdominal muscles more than any voluntary muscle in the body. Even upon lifting a light object, your abdominal muscles will tense moderately. In this way these muscles control most of your movements. By keeping some tension in the lower abdomen you are keeping in a ready position. Even though the rest of your body is relaxed, the slight abdominal tension will help assure a quick response to action.

Apply the practices of diagphragmatic breathing, breath rhythm and muscle relaxation in all of your daily activities. Coordinating all three initially requires concentration and will take time to feel natural. The most common obstacle confronted in the peak physiology exercises is the timing of the breathing pattern. If this is new to you it will take some practice to determine the proper pattern for optimal performance and rhythm. Most practitioners find that after several weeks of practice something *clicks* and the breathing pattern and timing all seem to fall in place naturally.

Performance

through focus

Throughout my early martial arts training, my instructor made a point of consistently stressing the importance of proper focus. He tends to teach lessons in ways not soon forgotten. I recall demonstrating a kata in front of the class when suddenly I felt the familiar rap of my sensei's hand on the back of my head. "Focus, more focus!" he bellowed in my ear. His commands urged me to perform my techniques with more vigor and force, concentrating intently on throwing each punch and block with all of my might. Meanwhile my instructor slipped behind me and artfully swept my back leg, tumbling me to the floor. "No focus" he chastised.

The concept of focus is regarded as one of the key compo-nents to proper martial arts practice. Kata competitions are lost because of techniques executed without focus. Techniques performed without focus during point sparring are deemed ineffective. Although most martial artists would agree with these assertions, few agree on the exact definition of focus or how to develop it.

When contemplating the concept of focus as applied to the martial arts, once again we are thrown headlong into the dichotomy between Eastern and Western thought. Western thought tends to define focus as a state stemming from deep, convergent concen-tration. Focusing on a issue usually connotes analyzing. Western analysis entails the process of fragmenting concepts into smaller parts to be assessed and more easily integrated. For example, when Western society *focuses* on a complex problem, the problem is divided into is sub-components to be examined more in depth. Possible solutions are then applied to each sub-component prior to once again looking at the situation from the broader perspective. This is the way we learn complex athletic routines such as kata. The kata is broken down into individual steps making it easier to integrate into our memory and nervous system. The steps are then re-synthesized back into the complete form.

Eastern focus approaches problems from more of a holistic, indivisible context. This orientation is particularly necessary when dealing with intricate physical activities requiring balance. A good example of this would be riding a bicycle. When learning to perform this complex physical action, it is quite difficult to break it into stepwise, intellectually processed chunks. If the entire process is not taken as a whole with all components of balance, steering, and peddling performed simultaneously, the action cannot be performed. The execution must be approached as a single unit. This is also how kata should be presented in the final result. Instead of a set of individual techniques strung together, it should be performed as a flowing process connected from beginning to end. So where is the focus? On each individual action or on the entire kata?

To approach this dilemma requires a shift in perspective away from the analytical process. In fact, the constant, dissecting analysis of the intellect only serves to inhibit physical performance and put the brakes on the flow state. This is not to say that analysis does not have its place in the martial arts. In the next two sections, we will examine the intellectual, left brain aspects of mental focus and how to constructively apply analysis to your athletic pursuits.

Action Questions

Analytical reflection is the heritage of the Western mind. Most of us have a constant, running commentary in our head that tends to judge everything that crosses its path. Our brains ask of every development, "Is it harmful, beneficial or not worthy of our attention at all?" Periodic reflection is an integral part of any training regimen. You must always review your goals to evaluate your progress as well as to judge the efficacy of your current training regimens. Everyone does this in one fashion or another. Unfortunately, athletes often approach self evaluation by using devitalizing questions. For example, when an athlete is performing poorly, out of frustration he may ask himself "Why can't I get this technique" or "Why am I so clumsy?" The answers to these questions will not support him - they will only serve to intensify his frustration. The answers to these questions lack the call to action that can solve the problem. I believe this tendency toward such questions is ingrained in all of us. In Western society we learn primarily by criticism and correction, therefore it is only natural that we have incorporated this approach to learning into our self evaluation.

The proper way to evaluate goals and performance is through nonjudgemental, action inducing questions. I call these *Action* questions. For example, instead of being critical of a technique that you did not perform as well as you could have, catch yourself and ask "What is the best way that I can improve on this technique?" "What if I shift my weight forward during the execution?" Ask only questions that direct your attention toward action that promotes progress and a resolution to the difficulty at hand. Don't get caught up in self criticism or self pity for making mistakes. Inner criticism only results in unproductive physiology that in turn perpetuates poor performance.

Every practitioner has occasions when they are performing far below their abilities. It is the sensation of "being off" that takes the joy away from training. Very little is accomplished in such a state. It is important to redirect your physiology and mental state when such occasions arise. Continuing to train in this spirit only further ingrains the pattern into your nervous system ensuring that the unwanted state will make reappearances on a regular basis.

When not performing well you need to *take action.* First, stop your current unproductive activity (assuming that you are not actively engaged in sparring) and change to your peak physiology as taught in Chapter Two. Once you are relaxed and taking deep abdominal breaths, you may ask yourself something like "What action can I take to get back to a beneficial workout?" Whatever question you ask, make certain that it provokes a positive action that will assist in solving the difficulty. Relax and let the question sink in for a moment. If you ask with the full intention of receiving a response, soon ideas and answers will be begin to emerge.

Perhaps some of the exercises in this book may come to mind. Perhaps you may become aware that you have been experiencing low energy because your diet has been poor and you require more healthful foods. Often just the act of asking an *action* question can break the counterproductive pattern with a perceptual change in your frame of mind leading to a more productive workout.

Exercise 3A
Action Questions

Work on creating the habit of evaluating your goals and performance using questions that require *action*. *Action* questions act as the catalyst to promote progress towards your goal. Always ask with the full intention of receiving an answer and answers will appear. Always be *Action* oriented.

Self Talk

I frequently hear athletes talking to themselves saying such things as "I can't believe I did that" or "you loser!" Negative internal dialogue plagues all of us at one time or another. Doubts creep in and your critical internal judge begins to tear away at your self-esteem. Athletes fail to realize how much negativity is reinforced into their physiology by allowing such negative self talk. Internal dialogue is the springboard from which your physical actions are launched. Negative self talk can sabotage physical performance in an instant. It only takes a moment of doubt while performing a complex technique to cause an increase in muscle tension, turning a flowing performance into a catastrophe.

For most athletes, self talk is a string of spontaneous, unsolicited judgements of how they see themselves in relation to their current situation. As with habitual questions, most athletes tend to dwell on self deprecating thoughts that sabotage performance. This pattern emerges from the framework of learning by criticism and correction. Most top athletes have escaped this detrimental practice. Champions don't continually bombard themselves with inner criticism that stifles potential. Through either spontaneous or intentional conditioning, top performers consistently engage in self talk that is conducive to success. To elicit your best effort, you must learn to mentally perceive and respond to athletic conditions like a winner.

The inner judge that evaluates your performance reinforces your belief system. If you doubt your abilities on a conscious or subconscious level, your doubts will pop up in your internal dialogue at the most inopportune time. Your doubts can literally talk yourself out of what you want. A single detrimental belief will grow and be reinforced by negative internal dialogue unless you make a concentrated effort to stop the process at the outset.

As soon as a negative thought arises, *change your physiology.* Stand tall, breathe deeply, shake your head, slap your thigh whatever it takes to shake off the negative feelings. Next, replace the negative thought with a positive, empowering statement, an affirmation. An affirmation is a preset, positive statement that you repeat mentally or out loud. These statements serve to program the mind towards peak performance while simultaneously blocking negative thoughts and criticisms from arising. As you continually repeat the affirmation, its message will eventually be taken into the subconscious mind as truth, triggering a corresponding improvement in performance. Many athletes attest to the positive benefits of affirmations when they are used properly and consistently.

There are four rules to making affirmations effective:

Rule one: The affirmation should be a short, positive, statement. Keeping the statement short allows for easier integration into the subconscious. Short statements are also easier to remember in times of maximal physical and mental stress. Always form the statement in the positive. If you say "I will not be weak and fearful," at some level your subconscious recognizes that you are thinking about being weak and fearful. A better choice would be "I am strong and confident."

Rule two: Form the affirmation in the present tense. Begin the statement with "I am" rather than "I will be." The only reality for the subconscious mind is the present. "Will be" is a future that may never arrive.

Rule three: Be consistent and repeat the affirmation often. It is best to stick to one or two primary affirmations to repeat frequently than to have many different statements. A consistent message is much more likely to imprint in your consciousness.

Rule four: Use language that is motivating to you. Use words that emote strong feelings. Instead of "I am strong and confident," someone may prefer "I am powerful and in control." After forming your affirmation, say it with emotion and commitment while being aware of inner sensations it evokes. Does it elicit feelings of excitement or inspiration? Each person's motivation is different so choose your own words carefully.

Affirmations in Action

While in college I attended a tournament with a friend who was participating in kumite. His affirmation at that time was "I am strong and unbeatable." During his kumite matches I could sometimes see him silently mouthing these words to himself. Unfortunately, his new girlfriend also attended the tournament. Despite his affirmation, much of his attention was on impressing his girlfriend. Although continually repeated, the affirmation did not transform into a change in physiology. With scattered attention bouncing between his girlfriend, his affirmation and his kumite match, my distracted friend was soundly defeated and did not perform near to his potential. Simply repeating affirmations like a parrot will not produce change. The affirmations must be ingrained with commitment and feeling.

Positive self talk, reinforced by commitment, leads to improved performance.

Exercise 3B
Affirmations

Reflect on what motivates you in your art and choose words that characterize this motivation to form positive affirmations. Follow the rules listed in this chapter when creating the affirmations. For the next thirty days, repeat the affirmations while en route to the training hall or during breaks while training. You may also try repeating the affirmations prior to going to bed at night and first thing in the morning. Keep all self talk positive!

One Pointed Attention

Affirmations are as far as most Western athletes go into mind-body training. Although affirmations can be helpful in improving performance through building confidence, I believe that the flow state is unreachable through only utilizing such acts of discursive thinking. Whenever a thought is present, even if it is a positive thought, the mind focuses partially on the thought and away from the current physical action. Therefore I recommend using affirmations *prior to* the workout - while en route to the training hall or just before a competition. When the mind is fragmented, thinking about something other than the current activity, this detracts attention from the present action. The essential requirement of attaining the flow state while actively engaged in a physical endeavor is true one pointed attention.

One pointed attention occurs when you are totally immersed in the current action. All discursive thought fades into the background and only the present experience exists. It is this quality of complete focus that allows you to perform at your best. One pointed attention directs all of your physical and mental resources to the task at hand.

How can such a state be reached? In American sports, many coaches seem to believe that anger will trigger peak performance. They attempt to goad their athletes into a frenzy of anger against their opponents using such phrases as "crushem" and "killem." While anger may result in a brief explosion of adrenaline, it cannot last long. Intense anger is a very difficult and energy consuming emotion to maintain. If prolonged, it actually weakens the athlete.

Another route which is prevalent in today's sports psychology is to access the feelings from past peak performances. This entails reliving a past peak athletic experience in which you may have performed fluidly and spontaneously or may have succeeded against the odds. You dwell on the past experience in hopes of recapturing the physical and mental sensations or quality of the experience. This strategy may work well for recreating a particular impression, however, because it draws attention away from the current action, I would not recommend it be used while actively engaged in physical pursuits.

Western sports traditionally train in ways that do not promote the flow state. Yet all of us have experienced it at one time or another. The first concept encountered on the mental path to the flow state is that of natural action. A good example of natural action is when a mosquito lands on your arm while you are otherwise occupied, such as while reading a book. Your hand has usually swatted the mosquito before the word "mosquito" flashes across your consciousness. Your body acted on your intention before your mind had time to reflect on it. This type of natural action usually carries a sensation of effortlessness with it.

At this point questions usually arise such as "How can you understand and respond without thinking?" In reality we do this all of the time. You constantly receive information through your physical senses that you intuitively know the meaning of without verbally expressing in your mind. For example, you walk outside to your car to go to work one morning and the word "umbrella" suddenly comes to you. You then go back inside to retrieve your umbrella. While not consciously aware, you had received physical signals such as moisture in the air and clouds that you interpret as the possibility of rain. You simply skipped the step of thinking "Gee, it looks like rain, better get my umbrella." This absence of reflection is the ingredient which raises your level of martial arts performance towards your potential.

Whenever your intention is separated from a physical action by an active thought or reflection, the action loses its spontaneity and "naturalness." Conscious decision making inhibits reflexive instinct. When a technique is executed from the point of reflection, it is often slow and telegraphed. The act of reflection redirects your attention momentarily away from the technique and in the process the technique loses some of its fluidity. When intention and action are connected, you will have the sensation as if the techniques are almost performing themselves! When engaged in sparring and there is an opening in your opponent's guard for a backfist strike, your hand should be headed for its target well before you mentally acknowledge the opening - just as the mosquito was swatted in the previous example.

The marriage of intention and action without intervening reflection is a truly extraordinary experience to have. If you regularly watch sports on television, you have probably witnessed the effects of such an experience on professional athletes. After a flawless performance, the sports commentators ask the athlete to comment on certain areas of their performance. The athlete seems to draw a blank for a moment and you can see the wheels of their mind furiously turning. They have to reflect on what they have accomplished for it was initially done without reflection.

This state of naturalness is akin to Zen concepts of "no mind" as well as other selfless states that are so much a part of the Eastern traditions. Fortunately you do not have to go to a monastery and meditate for ten years to accomplish this state. To attain this quality of awareness, one must simply be able to stop the endless analyzing and reflection that we have trained our minds to perform. We must train our attention to stay on the present action. While this is an easily understood teaching, it requires practice and discipline to develop this special quality of attention.

One pointed attention is essential when working with weapons.

Listening to the Body

Thought is almost always in the past or the future. We are either reliving situations in the past or deciding what to do in the future. The mind is virtually never in the present when actively engaged in reflection. In contrast, our bodies remain forever in the present. Where else is there for the body to be? Therefore to focus on present action it is most advantageous to place your attention on the physical.

There are numerous ways to accomplish this process. I prefer the approach known as *listening to the body*. Body listening is the process by which you simply notice how your body feels. You sense your body's presence in relation to the surroundings. You may place your attention on the cool air touching your forehead. You may take note of your breathing, the floor against your feet, or merely feel the movement of your muscles as you practice your art. It really does not matter which physical attribute you choose, as long as your attention remains there. I tend to prefer placing my attention on my breathing rhythm. When taking full, diaphragmatic breaths in a constant rhythm, the other aspects of peak mind-body physiology tend to fall into place automatically.

Notice I have stated that you *place* your attention and not *think* about the physical. This does not involve active cognition. You must simply be aware of these sensations and keep totally grounded in the physical moment. It is strictly a process of observing. No judging, worrying, anger or fear to distract you from your art. In this space lies the flow state. Here you will find your optimal performance unimpeded by the distractions of thought. In this space you can glimpse your true potential.

This is a radical shift of attention for most martial artists. While sparring, where does your attention usually reside? Why, on your opponent of course. Bringing awareness primarily to your own body rather than concentrating on your opponents actions will at first seem quite dangerous. The advantage realized by this approach is that you will *respond* to your opponents reactions rather than *react*. Body listening frees you from the entanglements of your inner dialogue that detract from performance. Attention on your own physical sensations brings proper action.

During episodes of anxiety and fear, particularly during events of physical confrontation, is when the technique of body listening is put to the test. When events distract you, and they will, the resulting thought will erect a barrier to spontaneous action.

Attention is like as muscle. As you exercise it, you will find your attention becomes stronger and can be maintained without distraction for longer periods of time. When distracting thoughts arise, try exhaling. Use the exhale as a signal to release the intervening thought with the breath and purge your mind of the distraction. The attention is then immediately returned to body listening. Be aware of what features draw attention away from body listening. It may be negative self talk, muscle tension, personal worries or thoughts of how others perceive you. Record the distractions in your training journal. Often just the awareness of the recurring intrusions helps to prevent them in the future.

As you progress with the technique of body listening, you will notice that you acquire more insight into athletic situations. You develop intuition so that you instinctively know what to do next. When sparring, you may suddenly know that your opponent is going to execute a roundhouse kick with his left leg. No reasoning is involved in this insight, you are simply in tune with the situation. Your subconscious mind recognizes the clues just as it recognized the impending rain or the mosquito in the previous examples. Cultivating athletic intuition is one of the greatest benefits of one pointed attention.

In mind-body training, we use the attention of the mind to guide the body while *simultaneously* using the body to control the mind. The flow state must be a cooperative venture between mind and body. As your ability to concentrate on kinesthetic input improves, you begin to become aware of how your thoughts and emotions affect your body. As fear or anger arises, you will immediately see the resulting tension appear in your body. Through listening to the body, you can program your mind to seek out and let go any unwanted tension in the muscles. Fear and anger cannot exist in a calm, relaxed body. As more awareness is cultivated, you will find yourself discovering and releasing more and more subtle layers of muscular tension that impede the power and speed of your actions.

Some martial artists are able to adapt quickly to these techniques while others take weeks or even months for this approach to feel natural. In the beginning, you may sense that you are performing poorly. You may experience feelings of being excessively tense and slow. In reality, this tension was always present, only now you have become aware of it.

When the steps outlined in this text are followed closely, practitioners begin to experience natural action on a regular basis. With time and practice, this will progress to true one pointed attention. I have found it very helpful to be well acquainted with the physical components of the flow state presented in Chapter Two prior to attempting the *body listening* exercises. By achieving the desired physical state of relaxation and breath control, your focus of attention naturally resides in the present activity. It is this one pointed attention that is the true experience of focus which one must achieve to reach the highest levels of performance.

Exercise 3C
Body Listening

Practice the art of listening to the body. Keep your attention on *the feeling* of your physical movements during training. Try to notice when and where tension arises in certain emotional or intense situations. Attempt to exhale and release the tension as soon as it is recognized. Be mindful of your physicalness not only during training but throughout the day.

Practice the art of body listening in every movement.

Performance

through visualization

No single strategy has changed the face of athletic training regimens more than the technique of visual imagery. Over the past twenty years, mental imaging has become an important tool used by nearly every world class competitive sport training program. The techniques were originally developed for athletic training by the Soviet Union and the Eastern block Olympic programs. The successes of the Eastern block countries in Olympic competitions during the 1970's generated enormous worldwide interest in these strategies. With time, the Soviet training programs were revealed to the West and slowly integrated into virtually every aspect of sports preparation. Unfortunately, the martial arts have yet to fully embrace this mental technology. Although some may exist, I have yet to visit a training hall where visualization techniques are routinely utilized.

My early martial arts training was straight from the "old school" - hours of deep stances, hundreds of kicks and buckets of sweat. Visualization exercises were not regarded as true training. My view of mental imagery changed after reading accounts of astonishing accomplishments attributed solely to visualization techniques. There are stories of prisoners of war teaching themselves how to play golf in their three foot by five foot cells using mental rehearsal while never picking up a golf club. In the 1970's, scientific studies began to appear. In one study, basketball players were found to improve their game equally by physical practice or by mental rehearsal. Over the past fifteen years, numerous medical studies have arisen demonstrating the positive effects of visualization on health as well as effects on autonomic physical functions previously thought to be beyond the control of the conscious mind. Vivid visualization affects pulse, skin temperature, stomach acid secretion and certain components of the immune system.

Visualization techniques are powerful because the mind does not distinguish between what is vividly visualized and what is done in physical reality. When actions are clearly visualized, neuro-physiologic pathways are formed just as though you were physically performing the action. The same neurotransmitters travel to the same muscles, often at sub threshold levels, resulting in muscle contractions only detectable by EMG monitoring. This process effectively tattoos the physical action into your physiology with subsequent improvement in your abilities. The results are comparable to physical training in experienced athletes.

There are several advantages to mental rehearsal. First, it can be done any time you have a few quiet moments. No equipment is required and no facility is needed. Second, you can practice your techniques mentally with perfect form every time. There is no limit to what you can experience in your mind. Third, it may be utilized during periods of injury to help maintain your performance level.

Effective visualization is not just daydreaming or random thoughts of training. There must be structure to the imagery and for maximal effectiveness, several ingredients must be present.

Relaxation

The first prerequisite for effective visualization is a relaxed, tension free body. The process of mental rehearsal is a function of the right brain. The right brain is the screen for mental imagery - it is responsible for the intuition, spatial relationships and athletic coordination which constitute the necessary skills of the martial artist. Access to the right brain can only be accomplished in a state of relaxation.

When deeply relaxed, brain wave patterns actually change. Deep relaxation is associated with a wave form termed alpha. Normally in every day activity, we live in a beta wave form state. The beta wave form is associated with left brain activity while the alpha state is the gateway to the right brain. We must tap the right brain for successful visual imagery training. Unfortunately for the martial artist, the left brain can easily override the efforts to access the right brain. Linear logic, anger and tension engage left brain functions that inhibit right brain receptivity. Clenched fisted, tight jawed determination will not work with mental imagery. The right brain hemisphere, as with athletic endeavors in general, functions best in the relaxed state. For the neuro-physiologic pathways to be imprinted by right brain mental imagery, the body must be free of significant tension. The relaxation exercise introduced in Chapter Two is a prerequisite to proceeding with mental rehearsal techniques.

Prior to visualization training, make yourself comfortable and close your eyes. Take a few deep, diaphragmatic breaths and let go of any stored tension with each exhalation. Next, concentrate on your face and forehead. Tense the muscles in this area firmly for five seconds and then relax. Do this with all of your muscle groups from head to toe as taught in Chapter Two. The process may take ten to fifteen minutes at first. As your proficiency increases you will find the time required shorten to as little as thirty seconds. If you still have problems attaining deep relaxation, continue this exercise for several days prior to proceeding to the visualization lessons.

Relaxation is the first step toward effective visualization.

Precision

For effective visualization you must have a clear, precise picture of the desired result. This is simply an example of "what you see is what you get." If you have fuzzy pictures you will have fuzzy results. Ambiguity is the enemy of successful mental imagery. If you hope to give your physiology commands that can translate into improved performance, sharp images are required. Visualizing with clarity takes some practice. Although everyone visualizes to some extent, those not practiced in visual imagery often find it difficult to maintain distinct, sharp, images for any length of time.

Clear, distinct images of every motion and body position are the key to success. Imaging exactly how your foot is turned or the angle of your arm can make all the difference. A highly detailed mental rehearsal provides precise information concerning physical adjustments for balance and body position required for proper execution of the technique.

Start with one element of a visualization. After you have gone through the relaxation exercise, visualize yourself performing a side kick. Concentrate your attention on how your supporting foot is placed on the floor. Look at the angle of the foot while the technique is performed. Is your heel flat on the floor or raised? After you have visualized this clearly, move on to another aspect of the technique such as how your hip rotates and your shoulders move. Then watch several aspects of the performance together. With practice you will soon visualize the entire technique in a detail and clarity that will astound you.

Moving Holograms

The mental pictures created during visualization should be three dimensional with movement. Just as reality is three dimensional, so should your mental rehearsal. It is easiest for most people to initially observe the performance of the technique from the third person point of view. Examine the action as if you are positioned on a camera crane just like a Hollywood director making a motion picture. View the picture from every angle, taking note of every detail of the performance. Visualizing the movement in three dimensions is difficult for some, but adding depth to the images increases the usefulness of the exercise tenfold. It is just a matter of training your right brain, which takes practice. You want to visualize an image just like a hologram, with the perspectives of length, width and depth all present to examine.

When most students first begin to visualize, they tend to produce still pictures of various poses. If visualizing a side kick, many students only see the image of the leg fully extended with the foot at head level. A Kodak moment to be sure, however not that useful for improving your technique. Remember, *what you see is what you get*. Imaging frozen postures does not imprint any action into the physiology. Imaging choppy movements produces choppy physical results. The image must be fluid in motion if you wish to produce fluid techniques.

By studying moving holographic images as a third party observer, your right brain can often work out complex logistics of balance and movement prior to even physically attempting the technique. For example, visualizing a spinning back kick from the spectator's point of view may give you the sensation of less than perfect balance. On further examination, you recognize that the angle of the supporting foot needs to be increased to achieve optimum balance. Visualizing the technique from only one position, in two dimensions or without motion would not provide you with this information. After you have witnessed the action from several vantage points, it is time to mentally rehearse the technique in the first person.

Visualize performing a technique from several angles.

Multiple Senses

The next step to mental rehearsal is to put yourself into the performance. Instead of viewing the action from a distance, you now execute the technique as if you were physically performing it. You move from the observer to the first person. To get the most from this exercise, use as many sensory modalities as possible. While most people are visually oriented, the images should not consist only of mental pictures. Experiencing the sensations in the muscles and tendons as the technique is performed may even be more important than visual imagery in imprinting the proper technique into the physiology.

I always stressed the visual aspect of imagery until I met a blind athlete who practiced mental rehearsal using only the sensory modalities that he possessed. Try to physically feel how your body would move and the tensions that would be present as if you were actually performing the technique. Hearing expected sounds such as cheers from the crowd, the snap of your gi or the sound of your kiai, all help to actualize the experience. Make the mental experience as tangible as possible by adding as many sensory details as possible.

Incorporate Feelings

Nothing can anchor an event into the mind better than strong emotion. Chances are that any event you remember with extreme clarity has strong emotion attached to it. What most people do not realize is that the event is not only anchored into the mind but the entire physiology. If you have a strong memory of a significant life event, you can recall not only the event but how your body felt at the time.

To get a strong feeling for the visualized technique, try varying the components of the mental movie. Turn up the lights making everything bright. Change the color of the scenery around you. How does this make you feel? Does different lighting or a specific color intensify the experience for you?

Now do the same with body sensations. Feel your muscles as you move through the mental rehearsal. When you feel that your real muscles are moving slightly, you've probably got it right. Sense the tension as you imagine the technique and vary it, creating more tension and energy, then relaxing and performing the technique more softly. How does this affect your experience? Then move on to sounds in the mental picture. Visualize performing the technique in total silence. How does that feel? Now add sound effects, the snap of your gi, the people around you, even your own breathing. Do these measures actualize the sensations more fully? Write down all of your findings in your training journal for future reference.

Every martial artist knows the feeling of performing a technique well; something just clicks and it feels right. Balance, coordination, and timing all come together, if only for a moment. This is the quality of sensation that you want to incorporate into your visualizations. The feelings can be of unstoppable power, control, joy, success or simply feelings of effortlessness. Any strong emotion will help to lay the neural pathways to imprint the technique in your physiology. Work with varying the sensory modalities of your visualizations until you have experienced the strongest possible positive impression.

These are the proper ingredients for effective visualization in a nutshell. It is extremely important to remember that mental rehearsal is a skill similar to physical training. Like any skill it requires time to master. Don't expect your initial attempt at visualization to be crystal clear images filled with detailed sensations. Your mind must be trained just as you train your body, with persistence and repetition. With repetition *you will see improvement* that will eventually be evident in your physical performance.

Effective Visualization:

1. Relax

2. Start simple, with a single element

3. Build in/combine individual elements to create a bigger picture

4. Create a moving hologram from the third person point of view

5. Move to the first person viewpoint

6. Experience all five senses

7. Incorporate emotions

Exercise 4A
Mental Rehearsal

Step One: Choose a comfortable place where you will not be disturbed for at least twenty minutes. While some people like to lie down while visualizing, I prefer a comfortable chair. Once comfortable, choose a technique you wish to improve. Start simple, with a single technique.

Step Two: Take three deep, diaphragmatic, relaxing breaths. With each breath, relax further. After three breaths take note of any tension in your body. When first beginning you may wish to start at the top of your head and go down through your forehead, face, neck. chest, etc., relaxing each muscle group as completely as possible.

Step Three: Once relaxed, imagine performing the technique you have chosen. Visualize yourself just as if you were watching a movie projected on the inside of your forehead. See yourself performing the technique perfectly from start to finish. Watch first from the front view, then from the side, the back, the opposite side and return to front view. Note how your feet are positioned, the angles of motion, the location of your center of gravity. Critique the technique. How can it be improved?

Now move to the first person and feel yourself performing the technique. Notice how your hands, hips and legs are moving together. Feel your center of gravity during the technique. Try to add sensations such as sounds and even smell to the visual image. Breathe from your abdomen using your chosen breathing pattern during mental rehearsal just as you would if you were physically performing the technique. If you make an error in the visualization, "rewind" back to the   mistake and correct it. Remember, you can pro-gram in mistakes as easily as correct technique so make certain the mental rehearsal goes just how you want it.

Run through the technique at least ten times paying attention to different details with each performance. Many athletes have difficulty maintaining focus on the visualization. Their minds ricochet from one thought to the next. If you run into problems keeping focused during the mental rehearsal, you may do better with a guided visualization. An example of guided visualization is provided in Appendix B.

Visualization During Injury

Most martial artists who have accomplished proficiency in their art have been plagued by injury at some time in their athletic career. Coping with the setback of injury can be one of the most difficult and frustrating times in training. Instead of passively giving in to injury, through visualization techniques you can not only maintain your skills but actually assist your body to heal.

In the 1970's, Dr. Carl Simonton began work applying visualization techniques in the treatment of cancer patients. Patients treated with standard medical treatment *and* imaging strategies often demonstrated a significantly better response than patients using standard therapies alone. The body responds to mental imagery. The same techniques can be utilized to facilitate recovery from athletic injuries.

Take for example, a martial artist with a knee injury. After going through the steps of relaxation, the athlete directs his attention on the injured area, initially just being aware of how it feels. First, concentrate on relaxing around the injury. Much of the pain from a musculoskeletal injury is from built up tension in the surrounding muscles. After relaxing around the injury, he may then imagine that the knee is enveloped by a warm, healing energy. He may choose to visualize the image of light, soothing rays of the sun warming the area. As the heat and light is imagined in the mind, the temperature of the area often increases due to blood capillary dilatation.

Another method of mental imagery is to characterize the pain and then create an imaginary antidote. For example, if the pain feels like a burning, hot coal, you may visualize ice water washing over the region, putting out the fire. Allow your own imagination to choose the proper image for healing.

After the healing visualization, begin to visualize events involving the rehabilitation of the injury. For a knee injury, you may visualize beginning to carefully stretch and work the injured leg. Then progress to imaging executing kicks at half strength, always with perfect technique. End with images of using the injured leg with perfect, powerful technique as you know you will perform in the future. Be sure to keep up your training journal during periods of injury just as if you were physically training.

Perform the healing visualization at least twice a day. Training through mental imagery will help to keep your athletic edge and your motivation to train during periods of injury.

Performance

through ritual

The preceding chapters have introduced a number of invaluable tools to help you attain your own peak performance state. You have now discovered the benefits of proper goal setting, managing your physiology, controlling your focus and training through visualization. You may have learned a new method of breathing, relieving muscle tension and a different way in which to focus your attention. Now is the time to put it all together.

Most experienced martial artists understand the elements of the peak performance state although few have made a study of it. A black belt knows the proper way to perform a technique. He understands the power of proper breath control and the importance of remaining tension free while executing techniques. Then why do all experienced martial artists not perform optimally with each endeavor?

Although many know the individual ingredients to peak performance, most lack the ability to have all the elements coordinated and working simultaneously. They concentrate on proper breath control then ignore the tension in their muscles. While relaxing the tension, they lose track of their breathing rhythm and timing. Difficulties arise because the techniques are approached solely from an intellectual standpoint. This approach simply does not work because the mind can only think of one thing at a time. What is required is one distinct stimulus that will trigger and coordinate all of the elements to create the peak performance state. This is the power of ritual.

Athletic endeavors are replete with habit and ritual. The tennis player bounces the ball the same number of times prior to each serve. The baseball player taps the dirt from his cleats in the exact same manner before stepping into the batters' box. Top martial artists tend to go through the same warm-up ritual prior to each competition. The purpose of these exercises is always the same. It is to ground the athlete in a certain mind-set, a state of optimal performance. Regrettably, these practices usually are borne from superstition or accidental habit rather than from purposeful training and only rarely produce the desired state.

Until recently, it was thought that optimal athletic performance could not be predictably reproduced on demand. The optimal performance state was believed to be something that just happened, as if by divine grace. After all, everyone has their good days and bad. As we have established, you cannot think of all the factors creating the peak performance state simultaneously and coordinate them by sheer will. Sports psychologists and behavioral therapists have found the key to this dilemma in pattern response conditioning. The same methods of conditioning that Pavlov used to condition his dogs are also effective for training athletes. As you may recall, Pavlov conditioned dogs to salivate whenever they heard a bell. He did this by continually ringing a bell (stimulus), while giving the dogs food. With time, the dogs became conditioned to salivate whenever they heard the bell whether food was present or not. The goal of this chapter is to guide you through your own conditioning process similar to Pavlov's dogs. You will create a distinct stimulus leading to your own unique peak performance state.

I have watched attempts at teaching conditioned rituals while attending a variety of athletic performance, business and health care related seminars over the years. The mistake most commonly made is that the instructors attempt to lead all the participants into the desired state using only the techniques, timing and stimuli that work for themselves. Only a very few benefit from this approach as it is not possible to mass produce such an individual response. Each person has their own nuances for what constitutes an effective ritual.

Creating Ritual from Memory

While the qualities that shape each person's peak performance state are indeed distinct, I can provide the *framework* to create your own ritual for peak performance. The first strategy for creating an effective ritual involves reproducing a particular mind state from memory. This entails conditioning the desired mind state to return on demand. The first step in this strategy is knowing the state you wish to attain. This is the hard part. You have to retrieve the features of a previous optimal athletic performance from memory.

Stop reading for a moment and recall a time when you were performing optimally - an occasion when you made training break-through is ideal. Hidden in this experience are the triggers that activate the optimal state. Your job is to investigate every detail of the experience. The exercises in Chapter Four can assist you.

What did you see during the experience? Picture it in your mind. Was the lighting bright or subdued? What colors were around you? Did you visually focus on anything in particular? What did you hear? Were there any sounds or specific words that inspired you? What did you feel? Was there tension in any particular muscle? How were you breathing? What was the temperature in the room? Note all of these sensations in your training manual for future reference.

If you are good at visualizing and retrieving specific data from your memory, you may sense that the state is being recreated by your recollections. Dwell on the quality of the experience, remembering every detail as vividly as possible, and attempt to intensify the sensations contained in the situation. This is not idle daydreaming but the intentional process of actively producing the desired state. When you feel connected to the experience and *feel* the quality of performing well, you are now ready to establish your ritual. While experiencing the desired mind state, elicit a distinct stimulus, one that you will eventually associate with this experience. The key to this type of conditioning is repetition, just like Pavlov's dogs. The stimulus may be something as simple as snapping your fingers in a certain way or touching the tips of your thumb and little finger. Choose the stimulus carefully. It must be an action that is comfortable and unmistakable. After several repetitions you need only to perform the stimulus and the state will be present. The neuro-physiologic association becomes imprinted.

Exercise 5A
Creating a Ritual

1.   Choose a stimulus that you wish to use to create your ritual. The stimulus should be something distinct, something that you do not do routinely. You may choose pressing thumb and forefinger together, pressing your thumb in the palm of your hand or tapping your heel hard against the floor. It can be one of your affirmations, said in a certain tone of voice. Be clear on your chosen stimulus before proceeding.

2.   Recall a time when you were performing superbly. Dwell deeply on the sensations of the experience. What did you see, feel, say to yourself, sense? How did you breathe? How did your muscles feel? F-e-e-l the confidence and the energy contained in your superb athletic performance.

3.   Now put yourself in the picture. Breathe the way you did then. Physically sense the muscle movement in the experience. Think the same thoughts associated with the peak experience. Mentally experience every sensation as if it was happening right at this moment. Be there, in your mind's eye.

4. As you generate this experience, feeling the attitude of performing superbly **and** sensing it in your body, perform your stimulus. Trigger your stimulus five or six times repeatedly while in this peak mind state. This process may need to be repeated several times before the trigger becomes established. Repeat this process until you can simply perform your chosen stimulus and automatically feel the quality of a peak performance.

Your ritual can be incorporated into your warm-up routine.

Creating Ritual in Training

Many athletes have difficulty recreating the ideal, peak performance state. The memories of the experience do not translate into a change in state.   For these people the ritual must be ingrained when actively training. When you are training and perform a technique so it feels *Perfect*, that is the state you wish to command. When you sense that you have entered into the flow state, stop for a moment and concentrate on that feeling. I am not talking about *How* you performed the technique but the *Feeling* of the state that allowed you to accomplish it. Perform your ritual trigger while concentrating on those sensations. Whatever the chosen stimulus, it must be repeated whenever you are performing optimally. Creating a ritual in this manner takes practice and patience. It may take several weeks to imprint the exact, desired training state to an effective ritual trigger. Don't give up if it doesn't work in the first few trials. The rewards of persevering are be well worth the effort.

Sequential Repetition

The third avenue for creating an effective ritual is through the sequential performance of the physical factors making up peak physiology. By taking the elements of peak performance you have learned in Chapter Two and mindfully going through each in sequence, the pattern becomes ingrained. For example, first concentrate on taking deep, diaphragmatic breaths followed by allowing your breath to settle into its natural rhythm. You must have already worked with your breathing pattern prior to this point. Once your breath is in rhythm, proceed with a scan of your body, relaxing all the muscles starting from the head down. Remember to leave a slight bit of tension in the lower abdomen in ready position. Continue to focus your attention on how your body feels, grounding yourself in your present action and in the present moment.

When you perform this ritual daily in the exact same order you will find that the pattern becomes ingrained so that when you take your first few diaphragmatic breaths, they trigger a cascade effect. Your breath will naturally fall into rhythm, your muscles will relax and your attention will be drawn to the present moment. Sequential repetition involves being mindful of your present activity instead of reliving past experiences or patiently waiting for peak performance to befall you. This is my preferred ritual and I have incorporated it into my warm-up/ stretch routine that I perform prior to each workout.

To create ritual in this manner requires the power of intention. You cannot just go through the motions. Each step must be performed attentively with the purpose of creating your desired performance state.

Ritual in Action

While in medical training, I would sometimes workout with an older gentleman who had taken up karate later in life. He was a physician, sixty-two years of age who suffered from debilitating arthritis in his hips and knees. Just watching him hobble along made me wince with empathic pain. Despite his disability, he trained four days a week, come hell or high water. Some days he could barely lift his legs to put on the pants of his gi. He would limp to the training mat to begin his warm up routine which he never varied. He began with yoga positions, holding each posture for ten seconds. With each posture he took deep, full breaths, concentrating fully on his uncooperative joints. This was followed by light stretching after which he would sit cross legged facing the wall with his eyes closed for two to five minutes. He would not speak during his routine. When he stood up to begin the workout, he was a different man. The limp was gone. His movements were fluid and agile. The few times we sparred I found him to be surprisingly quick and light on his feet. Following the workout he would nimbly jog to the shower. By the time that he dressed into his street clothes he had returned to his former self, once again stiff and restrained by his arthritis.

I often commented on his miraculous transformation and he would just laugh. On one occasion I jokingly accused him of taking some type of drug to which he replied "don't need to, I make my own." I believe in a way that this was a true statement. Something about his warm-up ritual drastically changed his physiology and ability, probably better than any pharmaceutical could have. It is the most convincing evidence of the power of ritual that I have ever witnessed.

Negative Rituals

While most athletes have to work at cultivating a beneficial ritual, we seem to have no problem attaining negative ones. It may start as something as simple as the thought "I'm feeling rather stiff today." Soon this leads to "my timing is off," and snowballs into "nothing is working right for me today." One negative thought allowed to settle soon has offspring. The key to transforming these detrimental occurrences is to watch your rituals closely, becoming aware of where each thought leads. Awareness is the key.

As soon as you begin to travel down the path of negativity, stop immediately and mentally shake off the negative sensations. Then, substitute your positive ritual. By observing sensations during your training, you can defeat negative rituals before they have a chance to start.

I have met martial artists who carry a variety of lucky charms with them to competition. Without them they feel helpless. Others feel that the weather and climate have to be a certain way for them to perform well. One competitor always kissed his wife prior to competition, without it he believed he didn't stand a chance. I disagree with giving the control of your ritual or trigger for optimal performance to external objects. It only disempowers yourself. I insist that my students throw away any restricting superstition and replace it with the knowledge that all the resources for peak performance are within themselves.

The most important part of creating a successful ritual is to keep your practice alive. The ritual needs to become an integral part of your training regimen. The ingredients of your ritual are not important. It is only important that you continually practice and allow the ritual to bring you back to an optimal performance state. Over time, a training habit forms that falls into place naturally and without conscious effort.

Consistent implementation of the techniques in this book can lead you to an optimal performance state at every workout.

Concluding Comments

If you have worked through the exercises in this text, you should have a good understanding of the optimum performance state for the martial artist and how to access it. Obviously the work is not over, in fact it has just begun. As you continue the journey of improving your art, refer to this book often. You may find that some element presented that you thought was minor during your first reading has now become quite important. As you progress, your understanding of the peak performance state will deepen leading to breakthroughs in performance. Your ability to relax while attending fully to the present action will bring greater satisfaction to your training and, most probably, to your life.

About the Author

Jacob H. Jordan, M.D. is a practicing surgeon and a lifelong martial artist. Based on his unique experience in both the medical arts and the martial arts, Dr. Jordan has spent over fifteen years applying health related mind-body research to peak performance training.

Appendix A

Your Training Journal

The importance of consistently keeping a training journal cannot be overemphasized. The training journal is the easiest method of keeping abreast of your progress and catching "bad habits" that hinder your success. In addition to recording your goals, motivation, training plans and time frame, the journal should include both your negative and positive impressions throughout the training process. These entries highlight the mental aspects of your training and point to areas requiring attention. Keeping a written training diary promotes the awareness that allows you to maintain control over the forces that direct and shape your goals.

I recommend making an entry into your journal at least once for each workout. The entries should be made either during or immediately following the training session. Emotions and insights that arise during training are short lived and often not well expressed if transcription is delayed until the next day when the events are just a memory. Cultivate the habit of keeping the journal easily accessible and using it often.

The journal should remain as private as a personal diary. You may not wish to accurately record your fears, weaknesses and concerns if you know they may be read by others. Privacy promotes honesty.

It is important that your journal also be a log of your set-backs. Did you encounter any negative internal dialogue during the workout? Did you have problems keeping you breathing rhythm with certain techniques? Did doubts about your abilities arise?

Suppose you are about to compete in a major tournament. Before, during and following the competition, pay attention to what goes on in your head and your body. What are you saying to yourself? Are you intimidated by other competitors? Are there areas of constant tension in your body? How is your breathing? Are the thoughts supporting you or fostering doubts? How did you feel during the competition? Confident and composed? Nervous and weak kneed? List what aspects of your performance worked well for you and which were disappointing. Be aware of both the positive and negative thoughts and feelings that occurred and postulate how they affected your physical performance.

Review the journal entries at least once every seven to fourteen days. Look for patterns - recurrent feelings and dialogue that support or stifle your abilities. Note when you feel powerful and when you feel unfocused and powerless. After several months it should become clear where your strengths and weaknesses lie. The process of recording your thoughts and impressions brings them into sharp focus allowing you to correct difficulties and bolster strengths.

Appendix B

Guided Visualization

If you are having difficulty with "free form" visualization, sometimes it is easier to tape a guided visualization. You can record a scenario to visualize on a cassette recorder and play it back to lead yourself through the mental rehearsal process. The steps to create your own guided visualization are as follows:

1. Choose the event to visualize. It may be a training session or a competition. Write in vivid detail all of the experiences you want to happen in the event from beginning to end.

2. Be descriptive, detailing every aspect of the event including the temperature, the sounds of other competitors and any other sensations that actualize the experience for you

3. Include your feelings of confidence and proficiency. This may include one or more of your affirmations interspersed with the action.

4. Edit your script, inserting words that inspire relaxation and confidence. Then, dictate the script slowly and deliberately into a cassette tape recorder. After you have gone through the steps of relaxation (which you may wish to record before your guided visualization), let your tape guide you in your mind's eye through the event.

The following is a sample guided visualization for a martial arts competition:

Begin with the progressive relaxation exercise detailed in Chapter 4. When relaxed;

Visualize yourself arriving at the location of the competition. See the building as you walk through the door. Notice the lighting, see and hear the other competitors as they warm-up.

Sense how you feel, you may recall an affirmation...I am relaxed and in control...I am a confident winner. Sense that you are feeling great and that it is a good day... feel your confidence. Begin your warm-up/stretch routine. Feel your muscles become loose and ready for action. Feel the floor as your feet presses up against it during the stretch. You execute a few warm-up punches and kicks sensing that you are unusually smooth and powerful today.   Sense the excitement of the coming event.

The sparring match begins..you are against a formidable opponent but you know that you are better. See your opponent - his stance - his size - the color of his eyes and hair.

Feel the slight tension in your abdominal muscles...the rhythm of your breathing...Your opponent executes a backfist that you easily block and counter with a lightening fast reverse punch to the head that scores. The referee signals a point for you.   You remain confident and calm as the match continues...The match continues and your techniques flow effortlessly as if pulled to their target by invisible strings. You are light, relaxed and your timing is in perfect synch with your breath. Experience your body sensations as you execute one technique after another, smoothly, gracefully, just as you had practiced them. Your body is unusually light and fluid. Enjoy the invigorating feelings of competition and the sensation of being at your best. As the match ends feel the sensation of being a winner and an accomplished martial artist. Feel the congratulatory pats on the back from your instructor and peers. Feel these positive impressions as you slowly leave the visualization and come back to your present surroundings.

Appendix C

Sample Affirmations

Some athletes have difficulty creating effective affirmations. Below are some sample affirmations. If these affirmations do not inspire you, you may tailor them by substituting language that is motivating for you.

General training

I am relaxed and in control

I am strong and powerful

I am a confident winner

I persist until success is mine

I love to push to expand my abilities

I stay in the moment

I pour my best effort into each activity

I remain relaxed and free from tension

I love my training sessions and I improve daily

I visualize to victory

I enjoy competing, it brings out my best

I am loose, light, and graceful

I stay healthy and strong

I create a great experience moment by moment

Specific affirmations for the martial artist

My kicks are fast as lightening

I perform kata with flowing, graceful power

My backfist is unstoppable

I am a master martial artist

I am a fearless, formidable opponent

I effortlessly master the techniques required for my ___belt

Glossary

antagonistic muscle opposing muscle in a limb that performs the opposite action; i.e. biceps vs. triceps

cc cubic centimeters, measure of volume

Chi life force energy (Chinese spelling)

diaphragm large, flat muscle separating the chest and abdominal cavities; the primary muscle of respiration

EMG electromyogram; the recording of changes in electric potential of a muscle

gi uniform worn by martial artists

karateka a practitioner of karate

kata a predetermined sequence of martial arts techniques

ki life force energy (Japanese spelling)

koan an unsolvable riddle used in Zen training to bypass the intellect and assist in achieving enlightenment

kinesthetic sensation of body position, presence, or movement

kumite free sparring

neuromuscular the muscle unit and the nerves that control its contraction

neurotransmitters substances that transmit impulses between nerve endings

parasympathetic component of the nervous system that slows heart rate; counteracts "fight or flight" response

physiology the characteristics of the processes, activities and functions of living organisms

psycho-physiologic the effect of mental processes and emotions on physiology

shorin-ryu a style of karate originating in Okinawa

sub-threshold below the levels needed for activation

sympathetic nervous system based on adrenaline; responsible for increased heart rate and "fight or flight" response

Taoist a practitioner of Taoism, a Chinese philosophy based on the teachings of Lao-tse

thoracic chest

Zen Japanese philosophy asserting that enlightenment can be attained through meditation, contemplation and intuition

Index

Other books available from Turtle Press:

Ultimate Fitness through Martial Arts
Teaching: The Way of the Master
The Art of Harmony
Taekwondo Kyorugi
A Guide to Rape Awareness and Prevention
Combat Strategy
Advanced Teaching Report
Launching a Martial Arts School
Hosting a Successful Martial Arts Tournament
Instructor's Guide to Ultimate Fitness
Coach's Guide to Taekwondo Kyorugi

For more information:

Turtle Press
PO Box 290206
Wethersfield CT 06129-0206
800-77-TURTL